The Intelli_____ Revolution: Unleashing the Power of AI in the ICT Frontier

Navigating the Intelligent Revolution in ICT with Artificial Intelligence Mastery

JAMES BRANDY

TABLE OF CONTENTS

TABLE OF CONTENTS

INTRODUCTION

CHAPTER ONE

CHAPTER TWO

The Impact of AI on ICT

CHAPTER THREE

The Impact of AI on ICT

CHAPTER FOUR

Building an AI-Ready Infrastructure

CHAPTER FIVE

AI in Network Security

CHAPTER SIX

Intelligent Automation in ICT Processes

CHAPTER SEVEN

Ethical Considerations in AI

CHAPTER EIGHT

The Future of AI in ICT

CHAPTER NINE

The Future Landscape of Intelligent Innovation

CONCLUSION

INTRODUCTION

In the rapidly evolving tapestry of technology, a revolution is underway—a revolution that transcends the boundaries of innovation and reshapes the very fabric of our digital existence. Welcome to "The Intelligent Revolution: Unleashing the Power of AI in the ICT Frontier." As we stand on the cusp of a transformative era, this book serves as your guide through the uncharted territories where artificial intelligence (AI) meets the vast expanse of Information and Communication Technology (ICT).

Charting the Course of the Intelligent Revolution

The intertwining narratives of AI and ICT have given rise to an epoch where intelligence is no longer confined to the realms of human cognition. Machines, endowed with the ability to learn, adapt, and make informed decisions, are ushering in an era that challenges the limits of what we once deemed possible. This book is a testament to the monumental shift occurring within the ICT frontier, where traditional paradigms are dismantled, and new possibilities emerge.

Unveiling the Power of AI

At the heart of this revolution lies the transformative power of AI—an omnipresent force that permeates every facet of the ICT landscape. From Understanding Machine Learning to delving into the intricacies of Neural Networks and Deep Learning, from deciphering the complexities of Natural Language Processing to unlocking the visual world through Computer Vision, each chapter is a revelation, uncovering the potential of AI to redefine how we process information, communicate, and shape the future.

Navigating the ICT Frontier

"The Intelligent Revolution" is more than a mere exploration of cutting-edge technologies; it is a roadmap for navigating the challenges and opportunities that lie ahead. Whether you are an industry professional seeking to harness the power of AI, a student aspiring to understand the foundations of intelligent systems, or an enthusiast curious about the future of technology, this book is your compass through the unexplored territories of the ICT frontier.

Embark on a Journey of Discovery

Join us as we embark on a journey of discovery—a journey that traverses the evolving landscape of ICT, unveils the rise of AI, and lays the foundations for an intelligent revolution. Together, we will unravel the complexities, envision the possibilities, and chart a course toward a future where intelligence and technology converge in unprecedented ways. Welcome to the dawn of "The AI Revolution. Navigating the ICT Frontier

"The Intelligent Revolution" is more than a mere exploration of cutting-edge technologies; it is a roadmap for navigating the challenges and opportunities that lie ahead. Whether you are an industry professional seeking to harness the power of AI, a student aspiring to understand the foundations of intelligent systems, or an enthusiast curious about the future of technology, this book is your compass through the unexplored territories of the ICT frontier.

Embark on a Journey of Discovery

Join us as we embark on a journey of discovery—a journey that traverses the evolving landscape of ICT, unveils the rise of AI, and lays the foundations for an intelligent revolution. Together, we will unravel the complexities, envision the possibilities, and chart a course toward a future where intelligence and technology converge in unprecedented ways. Welcome to the dawn of "The Intelligent Revolution.

CHAPTER ONE

In the ever-shifting terrain of Information and Communication Technology (ICT), the only constant is change. As we stand at the intersection of innovation and connectivity, witnessing the profound transformations in how we communicate, process information, and conduct business, it becomes imperative to comprehend the forces steering this evolution. This book embarks on a journey through the intricate layers of the ICT landscape, unraveling the threads that weave together the past, present, and future of this dynamic domain.

1.1 The Evolving Landscape of ICT

The first chapter delves into the metamorphosis of ICT, tracing its trajectory from its nascent stages to the present day. We explore the historical milestones, technological breakthroughs, and paradigm shifts that have sculpted the contours of this ever-evolving landscape. From the advent of the internet to the proliferation of mobile devices, each advancement has left an indelible mark on how we perceive and engage with information technology. Understanding this evolution is pivotal in navigating the challenges and opportunities that lie ahead.

1.2 The Rise of Artificial Intelligence

A beacon illuminating the path of this evolution is the ascension of Artificial Intelligence (AI). Chapter 1.2 unravels the narrative of AI's rise, examining its roots, breakthrough moments, and the pivotal role it plays in reshaping the ICT ecosystem. From machine learning algorithms that learn and adapt to neural networks simulating human cognition, AI has emerged as a transformative force. We explore the catalyzing factors propelling AI into the forefront of technological innovation and its implications for the broader ICT landscape.

Foundations of AI

The subsequent chapter delves into the building blocks of AI, laying the groundwork for a comprehensive understanding of its capabilities. From the fundamentals of machine learning to the intricate workings of neural networks and the realms of Natural Language Processing and Computer Vision, we embark on a journey through the core components that empower AI to redefine the boundaries of what is possible in ICT. As we navigate through these foundations, readers will gain insights into the mechanics driving AI applications and their potential to revolutionize the way we approach information and communication technologies.

Join us as we navigate through the nuances of the evolving ICT landscape, explore the meteoric rise of Artificial Intelligence, and lay the groundwork for a profound exploration of the Foundations of AI. The pages that follow promise a deeper comprehension of the technologies shaping our world and a roadmap for harnessing their power in the intelligent revolution that lies ahead.

CHAPTER TWO

The Impact of AI on ICT

In the ever-accelerating journey of technological innovation, Artificial Intelligence (AI) stands as a beacon, transforming the Information and Communication Technology (ICT) landscape. This chapter serves as a gateway into the profound impact AI has on ICT, exploring key facets such as Understanding Machine Learning, Neural Networks and Deep Learning, Natural Language Processing, and Computer Vision.

2.1 Understanding Machine Learning

At the heart of AI's prowess lies Machine Learning (ML), a discipline that empowers systems to learn and adapt without explicit programming. In this section, we embark on a journey to unravel the intricacies of ML, exploring its various paradigms—supervised, unsupervised, and reinforcement learning. Through real-world examples and practical insights, we demystify the algorithms that enable machines to recognize patterns, make predictions, and continuously enhance their performance.

2.2 Neural Networks and Deep Learning

Venturing deeper into the AI realm, we encounter the neural networks that emulate the intricate workings of the human brain. Deep Learning, a subset of ML, employs these neural networks to process vast amounts of data and extract meaningful insights. In this section, we dissect the architecture of neural networks, understanding how layers of interconnected nodes facilitate complex computations. As we unravel the layers of Deep Learning, we witness its transformative power in tasks ranging from image recognition to natural language understanding.

2.3 Natural Language Processing

Language, a cornerstone of human communication, becomes a realm conquered by machines through Natural Language Processing (NLP). In this segment, we explore how AI systems comprehend, interpret, and generate human language. From chatbots that engage in seamless conversations to language translation algorithms that bridge global communication, NLP exemplifies the marriage of AI and linguistic understanding. Unveiling the nuances of NLP opens the door to a world where machines not only understand words but also the context and sentiment behind them.

2.4 Computer Vision

The visual world, once exclusive to human perception, now becomes the canvas for machines through Computer Vision. This section delves into the algorithms and methodologies that enable computers to interpret visual information. From facial recognition to object detection, the applications of Computer Vision are vast and diverse. As we explore this facet of AI, we witness how machines gain the ability to "see" and interpret the visual cues that define our surroundings.

As we traverse the realms of Understanding Machine Learning, Neural Networks and Deep Learning, Natural Language Processing, and Computer Vision, the profound impact of AI on ICT becomes evident. These foundational elements not only shape the current landscape but also pave the way for a future where intelligent systems redefine the possibilities within the Information and Communication Technology domain. Join us as we unravel the intricacies and implications of AI, forging a path towards the intelligent revolution in ICT.

CHAPTER THREE

The Impact of AI on ICT

As we delve deeper into the symbiotic relationship between Artificial Intelligence (AI) and Information and Communication Technology (ICT), we enter a realm where the ripples of innovation transform into waves of unprecedented change. Chapter 3 unravels the multifaceted impact of AI on ICT, exploring Transformative Technologies, presenting Case Studies of Successful Integrations, and dissecting the myriad Challenges and Opportunities that emerge in this dynamic landscape.

3.1 Transformative Technologies

The pulse of the intelligent revolution lies in the transformative technologies that AI injects into the veins of ICT. In this section, we explore the groundbreaking advancements that redefine conventional practices. From autonomous systems that revolutionize transportation to smart cities that optimize urban living, the infusion of AI into ICT catalyzes a paradigm shift. We unravel the intricacies of these transformative technologies, peering into the future where AI becomes the driving force behind intelligent, interconnected ecosystems.

3.2 Case Studies: Successful Integrations

Real-world applications illuminate the path of theoretical possibilities, and in this section, we delve into Case Studies that showcase the seamless integration of AI into diverse ICT domains. From healthcare systems leveraging AI for diagnosis and treatment to financial institutions employing predictive analytics for risk management, each case study is a testament to the tangible impact AI has on enhancing efficiency, accuracy, and decision-making. Through these narratives, we glean insights into the strategies that underpin successful AI integrations, offering valuable lessons for industries poised on the brink of transformation.

3.3 Challenges and Opportunities

As with any revolutionary shift, challenges emerge alongside opportunities. This section dissects the nuanced landscape of Challenges and Opportunities presented by the symbiotic relationship between AI and ICT. We confront issues of ethics, privacy, and bias, acknowledging the responsibility that comes with unleashing intelligent systems into our daily lives. Simultaneously, we explore the vast opportunities for innovation, economic growth, and societal advancement that arise when we navigate these challenges with foresight and ethical considerations.

As we navigate through Transformative Technologies, explore Case Studies of Successful Integrations, and confront the myriad Challenges and Opportunities, it becomes evident that the impact of AI on ICT extends far beyond the realm of theoretical discourse. This chapter serves as a bridge between the theoretical underpinnings of AI and its tangible consequences, paving the way for a comprehensive understanding of the intelligence revolution that is reshaping the very foundations of Information and Communication Technology.

CHAPTER FOUR

Building an AI-Ready Infrastructure

In the fast-paced arena of Artificial Intelligence (AI), the potency of intelligent systems is not solely reliant on algorithms and models. Equally pivotal is the foundation upon which these systems are built—the infrastructure. Chapter 4 guides us through the essentials of crafting an AI-ready infrastructure, addressing critical aspects such as Hardware and Software Requirements, the synergy between Cloud Computing and AI, and the strategic considerations behind effective Data Management.

4.1 Hardware and Software Requirements

The engine that propels AI forward relies heavily on the capabilities of the hardware and the intricacies of the software it runs. In this section, we delve into the nuances of selecting the right hardware—whether it be GPUs optimized for parallel processing or specialized AI chips designed for intricate neural network computations. Concurrently, we explore the software landscape, from frameworks that facilitate model development to programming languages tailored for AI applications. Understanding the symbiotic relationship between hardware and software is fundamental to constructing an infrastructure capable of unleashing the full potential of AI.

4.2 Cloud Computing and AI

The marriage of AI and Cloud Computing is a transformative alliance that redefines how organizations approach infrastructure. In this segment, we dissect the synergies between Cloud Computing and AI, examining how the scalability, accessibility, and cost-efficiency of cloud platforms provide an optimal environment for AI deployment. We explore the services offered by major cloud providers, the potential for distributed computing, and the strategic considerations when deciding between on-premises infrastructure and cloud solutions. Navigating this landscape is crucial for organizations seeking to leverage AI without the constraints of traditional infrastructure limitations.

4.3 Data Management Strategies

In the realm of AI, data is not merely a byproduct but the lifeblood that nourishes intelligent systems. This section delves into Data Management Strategies, exploring how organizations can harness the vast troves of data at their disposal. From data acquisition and preprocessing to storage and retrieval, we dissect the intricacies of managing data for AI applications. We also address the importance of data quality, privacy considerations, and the emerging field of federated learning, where models are trained across decentralized data sources. Crafting an effective data management strategy is pivotal for building a resilient and adaptive AI infrastructure.

As we navigate through the intricacies of Hardware and Software Requirements, the symbiosis of Cloud Computing and AI, and the strategic considerations behind Data Management, we lay the groundwork for organizations seeking to establish an infrastructure capable of embracing the transformative power of AI. This chapter serves as a blueprint for constructing the backbone that not only supports intelligent systems but propels them towards new frontiers of capability and innovation.

CHAPTER FIVE

AI in Network Security

In the ever-expanding digital landscape, where connectivity is paramount, the role of Artificial Intelligence (AI) in fortifying network security has become indispensable. Chapter 5 delves into the domain of AI in Network Security, unraveling the intricacies of Threat Detection and Prevention, exploring AI-driven Cybersecurity Solutions, and addressing the imperative task of Securing the ICT Frontier.

5.1 Threat Detection and Prevention

As cyber threats become more sophisticated and dynamic, traditional security measures are rendered insufficient. In this section, we explore how AI becomes the guardian at the gate, capable of swiftly identifying and mitigating threats. From anomaly detection algorithms that discern unusual patterns of behavior to predictive models that anticipate potential vulnerabilities, AI is at the forefront of proactive threat detection and prevention. Understanding the role of AI in this context is pivotal for organizations seeking to fortify their defenses against an evolving cyber threat landscape.

5.2 AI-driven Cybersecurity Solutions

The arsenal of tools available for cybersecurity is expanding, with AI-driven solutions emerging as a potent force. This segment delves into the myriad ways in which AI augments cybersecurity efforts. From machine learning algorithms that continuously adapt to new threats to automated response systems that neutralize attacks in real time, AI is transforming how organizations safeguard their digital assets. We explore case studies and practical implementations, providing insights into the effectiveness of AI-driven cybersecurity solutions in diverse contexts.

5.3 Securing the ICT Frontier

As organizations embrace AI in network security, the holistic security of the Information and Communication Technology (ICT) frontier becomes paramount. In this final section, we address the broader considerations of securing the entire ICT ecosystem. We examine the integration of AI into endpoint security, cloud security, and the protection of critical infrastructure. Moreover, we explore the ethical implications of AI in cybersecurity, ensuring that the deployment of intelligent systems aligns with principles of privacy, transparency, and responsible use.

As we navigate through the realms of Threat Detection and Prevention, delve into AI-driven Cybersecurity Solutions, and address the imperative of Securing the ICT Frontier, this chapter serves as a comprehensive guide for organizations looking to fortify their digital perimeters. In the dynamic landscape of cyber threats, AI emerges not only as a guardian but as a proactive and adaptive force, reshaping how we approach the security challenges of the interconnected world.

CHAPTER SIX

Intelligent Automation in ICT Processes

In the pursuit of operational excellence and efficiency, organizations are turning to Intelligent Automation, where Artificial Intelligence (AI) takes center stage in reshaping Information and Communication Technology (ICT) processes. Chapter 6 navigates through the realms of enhancing efficiency with AI, exploring the landscape of Robotic Process Automation (RPA), and delving into the symbiotic relationship of human-AI collaboration.

6.1 Enhancing Efficiency with AI

Efficiency, the heartbeat of any thriving organization, finds a powerful ally in AI. In this section, we explore how intelligent automation elevates efficiency across diverse ICT processes. From streamlining data workflows to optimizing decision-making through predictive analytics, AI has become the driving force behind operational agility. We delve into case studies illustrating how organizations harness the power of AI to enhance efficiency, reduce costs, and propel their ICT processes into a new era of productivity.

6.2 Robotic Process Automation

The marriage of AI and robotics gives rise to Robotic Process Automation (RPA), a transformative force in the automation landscape. This segment dissects the intricacies of RPA, exploring how software robots mimic human actions to execute repetitive tasks seamlessly. We examine the implementation of RPA in ICT processes, from data entry to system monitoring, unraveling the potential for increased accuracy and operational speed. The discussion extends to the strategic considerations in adopting RPA and how organizations can leverage this technology to optimize their workflows.

6.3 Human-AI Collaboration

The future of intelligent automation isn't about replacing humans; it's about collaboration. In this final section, we explore the symbiotic relationship between humans and AI in the workplace. From decision support systems that augment human judgment to collaborative AI interfaces that enhance user experience, the collaboration between humans and AI transforms how ICT processes are executed. We delve into best practices for fostering this collaboration, ensuring that human creativity and critical thinking harmonize with the analytical power of AI.

As we navigate through the realms of enhancing efficiency with AI, explore the landscape of Robotic Process Automation, and understand the nuances of human-AI collaboration, this chapter serves as a guide for organizations seeking to revolutionize their ICT processes. Intelligent automation becomes not just a tool for efficiency but a catalyst for innovation, enabling organizations to thrive in the ever-evolving landscape of information and communication technologies.

CHAPTER SEVEN

Ethical Considerations in AI

In the age of Artificial Intelligence (AI) integration into Information and Communication Technology (ICT), ethical considerations become paramount. Chapter 7 delves into the nuanced aspects of ethics, addressing Bias and Fairness, delving into Transparency and Accountability, and exploring the intricacies of Ethical Decision-Making in AI applications.

7.1 Bias and Fairness

The specter of bias looms large in AI, reflecting the prejudices inherent in training data or algorithmic decision-making. In this section, we confront the challenges posed by bias and emphasize the critical importance of fairness in AI applications. We explore methods to identify and rectify bias, striving for equitable AI systems that serve diverse user groups without perpetuating discrimination. Understanding and mitigating bias is an essential step toward fostering an inclusive and just technological landscape.

7.2 Transparency and Accountability

Transparency is the cornerstone of responsible AI deployment. This segment scrutinizes the need for transparency in the decision-making processes of AI algorithms. We delve into methods to enhance the interpretability of AI systems, enabling users and stakeholders to understand how decisions are reached. Simultaneously, we emphasize accountability, exploring mechanisms to hold AI developers and organizations responsible for the outcomes of their intelligent systems. Transparency and accountability form the bedrock of ethical AI, ensuring that the technology aligns with societal values and expectations.

7.3 Ethical Decision-Making in AI Applications

As AI systems become increasingly autonomous, the need for ethical decision-making becomes more acute. In this section, we explore the ethical considerations that arise in the development and deployment of AI applications. From navigating privacy concerns to addressing the impact on employment and society, we delve into the ethical dimensions of AI decision-making. This exploration provides a roadmap for developers, policymakers, and organizations to navigate the complex landscape of ethical considerations in AI applications.

The Future of AI in ICT

As we traverse the ethical dimensions of Bias and Fairness, Transparency and Accountability, and Ethical Decision-Making, we gaze into the future. Chapter 8 paints a visionary landscape where AI reshapes the Information and Communication Technology (ICT) domain. Emerging trends, anticipated developments, and the potential societal impacts of AI are examined, providing insights into the trajectory of the intelligent revolution that lies ahead. Join us as we peer into the horizon of the future, where ethical considerations guide the evolution of AI in ICT.

CHAPTER EIGHT

The Future of AI in ICT

As the intelligent revolution in Information and Communication Technology (ICT) unfolds, Chapter 8 explores the dynamic landscape of the future. From Emerging Trends that shape the contours of tomorrow to Anticipating Technological Developments that push the boundaries of possibility, we embark on a journey to understand The Road Ahead in the ever-evolving synergy between Artificial Intelligence (AI) and ICT.

8.1 Emerging Trends

The landscape of AI in ICT is in perpetual flux, and emerging trends offer a glimpse into the future. In this section, we survey the cutting-edge developments that are poised to redefine the ICT ecosystem. From the convergence of AI with other transformative technologies to the rise of decentralized AI and edge computing, we explore the trends that hold the potential to revolutionize industries, reshape user experiences, and unlock new realms of innovation. Understanding these emerging trends is pivotal for organizations aiming to stay at the forefront of technological advancement.

8.2 Anticipating Technological Developments

The future is an unwritten canvas, and technological developments are the brushstrokes that paint the picture of tomorrow. This segment delves into the art of anticipation, exploring the technological developments that are on the horizon. From advancements in natural language processing and computer vision to breakthroughs in AI ethics and explainability, we unravel the threads of innovation that will weave the fabric of the future. Anticipating these developments is not merely a strategic advantage but a necessity for organizations seeking to harness the full potential of AI in ICT.

8.3 The Road Ahead: Implementing AI Strategies in Organizations

As we envision the future, the road ahead is illuminated by the implementation of AI strategies in organizations. This section serves as a practical guide, offering insights into crafting an AI adoption plan. From fostering a culture of innovation to overcoming resistance to change, we explore the strategies that organizations can employ to seamlessly integrate AI into their workflows. Success stories in AI integration provide inspiration, illustrating the tangible benefits of strategic implementation. The chapter concludes by providing a roadmap for organizations navigating the dynamic terrain of the intelligent revolution in ICT.

As we navigate through Emerging Trends, Anticipating Technological Developments, and The Road Ahead in Implementing AI Strategies in Organizations, this chapter serves as a compass for individuals, businesses, and policymakers. The future of AI in ICT is not a distant destination but a landscape shaped by our collective decisions and actions today. Join us in exploring the possibilities and challenges that lie on the road ahead, as we continue to unfold the narrative of the intelligent revolution.

CHAPTER NINE

The Future Landscape of Intelligent Innovation

In the concluding chapter of "The Intelligent Revolution: Unleashing the Power of AI in the ICT Frontier," we turn our attention to the future. The Intelligent Revolution is an ever-evolving journey, and as we stand at the threshold of what lies ahead, we explore the emerging trends, challenges, and opportunities that will shape the landscape of intelligent innovation in the years to come.

Section 1: Beyond Automation - Cognitive Empowerment

1.1 Moving Beyond Routine Tasks

Examining the evolution of AI from automating routine tasks to empowering individuals and organizations with cognitive capabilities. Discuss how AI will increasingly collaborate with humans to enhance decision-making, problem-solving, and creativity.

1.2 The Rise of Augmented Intelligence

Exploring the concept of augmented intelligence, where AI systems augment human capabilities rather than replace them. Discussing real-world examples of AI assisting professionals in various fields, from healthcare to finance.

Section 2: AI and Sustainable Development

2.1 Addressing Global Challenges

Investigating the role of AI in tackling pressing global challenges, including climate change, healthcare disparities, and poverty. Highlighting how intelligent technologies can contribute to sustainable development goals and foster positive societal impact.

2.2 Responsible Innovation for a Better World

Discussing the ethical imperative of incorporating responsible innovation practices into AI development. Emphasizing the need for global collaboration to ensure that AI solutions contribute to a more equitable and sustainable world.

Section 3: The Evolution of Human-Machine Collaboration

3.1 Seamless Human-Machine Interaction

Examining advancements in natural language processing, computer vision, and other AI technologies that contribute to more seamless interactions between humans and machines. Discussing the implications for user experience and the integration of AI into everyday life.

3.2 The Emergence of AI Ecosystems

Exploring the development of interconnected AI systems and platforms, creating ecosystems that enable collaboration and information sharing among diverse intelligent entities. Discussing the potential benefits and challenges associated with these evolving ecosystems.

Section 4: Overcoming Technical Challenges

4.1 Continual Advancements in AI Research

Examining ongoing developments in AI research and the technical challenges that researchers are working to overcome. Discussing breakthroughs in areas such as unsupervised learning, explainability, and the quest for artificial general intelligence.

4.2 Ethical AI as a Technical Imperative

Highlighting the integration of ethical considerations into the technical development of AI systems. Discussing how ethical AI principles can be embedded into the design, development, and deployment phases to ensure responsible and beneficial outcomes.

Section 5: The Role of Governments and Policies

5.1 Crafting Adaptive Policies

Discussing the crucial role of governments in shaping policies that foster innovation while safeguarding ethical considerations. Examining examples of AI regulations and standards that governments around the world are implementing to guide the responsible development and use of AI.

5.2 International Collaboration and Governance

Advocating for increased collaboration among nations to establish international norms and governance frameworks for AI. Discussing the challenges and opportunities associated with creating a global consensus on AI ethics and regulations.

CONCLUSION

In the concluding pages of "The Intelligent Revolution: Unleashing the Power of AI in the ICT Frontier," we reflect on the transformative journey we have undertaken through the realms of artificial intelligence, innovation, and the ever-expanding Information and Communication Technology (ICT) frontier. This exploration has been a testament to the incredible strides humanity has made in unleashing the power of intelligence, as well as a call to action for the responsible and ethical stewardship of these technologies.

Our journey has taken us through the genesis of intelligent systems, the societal implications of their deployment, and the intricate dance between humans and machines. We've explored the opportunities and challenges on the horizon, recognizing that the Intelligent Revolution is a dynamic force that requires continual vigilance, adaptability, and ethical commitment.
As we stand at the threshold of an intelligent future, several key themes emerge:

Empowerment through Collaboration

The true power of the Intelligent Revolution lies in the collaboration between humans and machines. Augmented intelligence, where AI systems enhance human capabilities, is not just a possibility but a reality shaping industries, creative endeavors, and our everyday lives. This collaboration empowers us to address complex challenges, drive innovation, and explore new frontiers that were once unimaginable.

Ethical Imperative

At the heart of the intelligent future is an unwavering commitment to ethics. The ethical imperative is not a checkbox but a continuous journey—a commitment to transparency, fairness, accountability, and the preservation of human dignity. It involves navigating uncharted ethical territories, addressing biases, and ensuring that the benefits of AI are shared equitably across societies.

Global Collaboration

The Intelligent Revolution transcends borders, demanding international collaboration. The establishment of global ethical standards, the sharing of knowledge and best practices, and collaborative governance are essential for navigating the complex challenges and opportunities that lie ahead. Together, we can shape a future where the benefits of intelligent technologies are accessible to all.

Lifelong Learning

As intelligent systems evolve, the need for lifelong learning becomes paramount. The journey doesn't end with the acquisition of knowledge but requires a continuous commitment to staying informed, adapting to new technologies, and fostering a culture of innovation and curiosity.

Responsible Innovation

The future is not predetermined; it is shaped by our collective actions today. Responsible innovation involves a delicate balance between pushing the boundaries of technology and safeguarding against unintended consequences. It requires ethical leadership, user-centric design, and a commitment to building a future that prioritizes the well-being of individuals and society.

In closing, the Intelligent Revolution is not just a technological evolution; it is a societal transformation that requires our collective wisdom, foresight, and compassion. As we embark on the next phase of this revolution, let us do so with a sense of responsibility, guided by ethical principles, and with a shared vision of harnessing the power of **ARTIFICIAL INTELLIGENCE** for the betterment of humanity.

May the Intelligent Revolution be a force that elevates us, empowers us, and enriches the tapestry of human existence. The future is intelligent, and it is within our hands to shape it wisely and with purpose.